BOOTSTRAP

*Start Where You Are With What You Have
& Successfully Scale Business*

Vikki Jones

VMH

VMH Vikki M. Hankins™ Publishing
www.vmhpublishing.com

Book Cover Design by Vikki Jones
Book Cover Image: Canva
Interior Design by Vikki Jones
Interior Images Photographed by Vikki Jones

VMH Vikki M. Hankins™ is a registered trademark, and
the publisher of this work. For information about special
discounts for bulk purchases, please contact Vikki M.
Hankins Publishing specials sales at
info@vmhpublishing.com.

Publisher's Note:

Manufactured in the United States of America

10 9 8 7 6 5 4 3 2 1

Hardback ISBN: 978-1-947928-47-3
Paperback ISBN: 978-1-947928-44-2
eBook: ASIN: B07K2NC79S

Have a great business idea but no capital? It's possible to build and grow a profitable business without external help or capital. With today's digital platforms and technology, a business can be established with little money.

I started my original idea for book publishing with only $50. This was just enough money to register my business under the fictitious name category. That $50, coupled with a donated laptop and flip phone led to bootstrapping business success.

I was inspired to write Bootstrap because of the amount of people that delay or do nothing about their idea(s) due the lack of working capital.

Within this book you will find the framework to start, build and scale a business successfully without tapping into another's bank account. Within this book you will find direct results of my bootstrapped work including A-List celebrities, A-List businesses, global influencers, and even a President of the United States. I started my company without funding, without capital, without anything. I had an idea, I had passion and I did something about it. I started where I was with what I had and successfully grew my company. If I did it, so can you!

"Bootstrapping a business can be scary...But many successful businesses are born this way without any help from external capital."

Shopify

BOOTSTRAP

Bootstrapping Reality

Bootstrapping is a different type of beast than raising money through investors to scale business. With both comes intense pressures, dedication and passion. Passion is the fuel for the success of your business.

I will not speak much on investor backing, funding, etc. however, I have this to say about seeking money to grow your idea or bring it to life.

Not everyone is given the opportunity to receive an advance or loans. Based on some of the statements made on the hot show, Shark Tank, an investor-based show with millionaire host/investors, oftentimes those with money are looking to make a quick return on the money invested. Of course there are several factors outside of quick returns that determine if investors will advance a few million or not but I've been on the receiving end of an investor advising me to seek out an angel for my idea. The recommended person was of my same race and I got the impression that I was more of a charity case than an actual businesswoman. Because of my business field perhaps my work is seen as some form of charity versus a tangible product. I do not know but what I did know was I wasn't going to wait around for someone to loan me money in order to move forward with my idea.

On a more plausible business side of investing, investors have to know you're scaling and making enough sales and that they can actually increase the sale of your products before putting their money and resources behind it.

Here is the thing with this process of looking for money to start, grow or better manage your idea. Simply put, you may not receive a dime from anyone. Whether it's for reasons of your skin color, no one believe in your idea, or you aren't making enough money for investors to make a fast return; what do you do if no one loans you funds?

There's a very strong possibility that some won't receive millions in the first round of seed funding. For startups like Uber, in my opinion   co-founder Travis Kalanick, who was giving *investors* an *opportunity* to make money through his idea. Based on my analysis, he was confident, knew he had a brilliant idea that would reinvent the way the world uses ground transportation. Enter technology and smartphones he knew he had a winner; the right connections, timing and access only added to a money-making formula for himself and investors.

I don't like to harp on race, gender and/or skin color but when the odds are against you – even though you know your product is a winner; when you are the only one who believes – do not waste your time trying to convince others to believe and invest their money in your idea. I don't care what color or gender you are.

The vision is yours to act on. Most won't see what you see in the beginning. To be frank, I think it was meant for others to turn a blind eye to my vision in order to develop my skills in creativity, marketing and sales in order to develop and learn new technologies.

It is harder when you don't have the resources and funding readily available to

you but certainly not impossible otherwise
I wouldn't be writing this book!

President Obama – Silicon Valley

The one thing I want to be clear about is that everything I'm about to say is solely and exclusively my opinion, my view, and my analysis based upon personal experiences and observations.

I saw and experienced something similar to a purpose-driven mission during the administration of President Barack Obama, particularly during his last year in office. This mission was inclusive to all people regardless of their skin color, gender, sexual preference, income status and more. It was inclusive in the area of entrepreneurship and business.

Based upon his public word, I always knew and could see that he was cut from a different cloth, showing no biases. In 2016 I miraculously experienced firsthand his passion to level the playing field and include people who were generally excluded.

The first thing that happened through his small business initiatives: I had the privilege of being on a phone call where President Obama spoke to entrepreneurs in the United States. For those on that phone call extra security measures were taken and his adviser Valerie Jarrett was also on that call at the end. He shared some of what he liked to see small business owners to be involved with, and what he envisioned for small businesses to have in terms of success. It was surreal to be on my cell phone with President Barack Obama on the other end. He was speaking to me. It was a big deal, huge! I shared it with my friends on Facebook and other social media platforms. I walked away from that phone call not only in disbelief but with a feeling as though somehow as a business person that my company had gone to another place.

Later that same year, 2016, the magazine and media portion of my company was selected as a delegate to participate in President Obama's Global Entrepreneurship Summit, which was held in Silicon Valley, California on the Campus of Stanford University. You couldn't buy a ticket to this event you had to be selected out of thousands of submissions to participate. I was stunned! My small media company was selected to cover this major event for entrepreneurs, hosted by the President of the United States.

Bloomberg was one of the main

media entities at this summit. And to think my publication, VMH magazine, an independent magazine that barely received an advertiser, was selected to participate. VMH covers events with the goal to get information out to small businesses and entrepreneurs. My small entity, independent privately owned, bootstrapped magazine and media company was selected.

One of the greatest things that impacted me about the summit was the lack of exclusion for people with brown, dark brown, light brown skin tones. I believed that if you were a person with brown skin you had a fair shot at pitching to investors, add interest in your company, and funding for your vision. Although I believed in equality, up to that time I had not seen or experienced that.

I started my company with book

publishing and moved the vision forward in 2008. The vision began in 2005 but implementing practical steps came in 2008. Up to that time I had not witnessed black and brown people included to that degree (President Obama's initiatives) in business. Outside of those who attended, the access and all the people around me impacted me more than anything else. I listened to President Obama talk about inclusion, diversity and fair shots. I witnessed it with my own eyeballs.

When I prepared for the trip in 2016, after being approved for President Obama's Global Entrepreneurship Summit, I packed my cameras, tripods, Macbook Pro, phone, iPad, and everything that I could carry. The equipment was heavy but I knew I needed it to do a quality job. I love using the technology that I purchased, that I bootstrapped, for my company. I have invested in the equipment, the technology, the digital platforms, the travel, the ground transportation, the hotels, my physical appearance all in order to help my company grow.

One of the things that happened as I readied for my trip from Atlanta, Georgia to California is that there was another opportunity, I always do research. I researched President Obama's travel to California to learn when he would be there. It was a three or four day event, which meant that he couldn't be there the entire time. I found that Palo Alto, California was preparing for his visit and reporters and media outlets were getting information out about his arrival. There was a news site for additional press/media that wanted to come out to where Air Force One was landing. Through that site, reporters and publishers were able to apply for media credentials.

While I was waiting to board my plane, I pulled out my Mac to do research. That was when I found the news piece about his arrival and media credential applications; I applied, just as we were to board the plane. There I was, trying pack up my laptop, unzip and zip my bag, run to board and not miss my flight. It came down to that zipper as I put my Macbook Pro back into my bag, packed my stuff together - this situation formed an idea for a new product.

I needed convenience, something that I could use when I have to work fast and use my computer, not my phone, return it to my bag and keep on the move. An idea was formed for a product. exclusively for women in tech who have to travel. A product for those who have to, for the most part, be a one-woman show while operating cameras, travelling, recording, speaking with folks and interviewing, taking pictures, videoing and having to look nice and move in a smooth way; where you're not looking chaotic in the process.

The day that President Obama was to arrive I received an email saying I was approved to go out to the military base and cover the event of his landing. Everyone around me at the Global Entrepreneurship Summit was trying to figure out how I got the extra media access with the President's arrival when they didn't. Well it was because of that last minute research before boarding for California.

Throughout this process of growing and believing in my company, without the funding of the backers, I've used incredible amounts of strategic thinking, digging, and researching. I took every second available, even at the last minute and that is how I did it, an unconventional approach versus the traditional way.

When I arrived at Palo Alto, I stayed in a hotel with a style I never experienced before. It did not matter to me; as long as I had a safe place to lay my head, to sleep, and I was close to the university, safety was most important, I was good. It was close to the university with easy ground transportation, I didn't necessarily have to take Uber. Stanford has convenient transportation for its students. When I went to pick up my media credentials, my name was there, my boyfriend's name was there (now he's my husband), but his name was there even though both of us couldn't afford to travel to that particular event.

Another thing that stood out to me, in addition to President Obama's inclusive practices, was at that no matter where I was in Stanford's proximity the internet was live. I didn't have to plug into a free WiFi spot, it was simply available on the streets. Standing up and I got Wifi. I was like what is going on? The other thing that stood out for me was that, I was able to actually see the brick and mortar buildings of the digital/tech platforms that I use for my company.

Seeing that connection was important for me. The digital magazine, VMH magazine and the digital platforms I have used were located in Palo Alto, California. To actually see the brick and mortar building where people were working to provide these digital platform services to folks across the country just made it very real for me. For some reason, I didn't think beyond the digital internet platform, I couldn't see brick and mortar in my mind's eye. I checked in, picked up my pass, had great food, everything was wonderful.

There were many people there from around the world and it was impressive, very impressive to see the CEO and co-founder of Uber, the co-founder of LinkedIn; the CEO of Google; the founder of Facebook, Daymond John of Shark Tank; Founder, Daniel Lubetzky of KIND Snacks; the head of the U.S. Small Business Administration, Maria Contreras-Sweet; the co-founder of BET networks, Sheila Crump Johnson; and so many people who started their business whose brands are utilized by so many people around the world. To be in that room to be in that space, to be able to talk with these people, interview these people, photograph these people, associate with them, all because President Barack Obama determined that race, gender, income status, or culture would have no bearings on entrepreneurs who worked toward their vision.

In anything that is great, often times you are going to find challenges you are going to find obstacles, you are going to find folks that literally slam the door in your face, or maybe even see you as despicable for no reason at all. Other than something that they had yet to deal with. Such as the case with me of two people that I encountered during this amazing summit.

One person did not want me to go in the room, the space where President Barack Obama was giving his speech, or former senator John Kerry or all the other fascinating people. The woman blatantly told me that I would not be going into that particular room or that particular space. Only a select few would. According to this situation, I was not chosen to go in there where President Obama would be there. I couldn't believe it. It wasn't that I wasn't chosen that I couldn't believe but it was her demeanor that I didn't understand. Why it felt like she had such a loathing towards me. I didn't know this woman. But here's the interesting thing, that same woman had to come back in that room where we were sat, waiting to see who would actually go into this space where President Obama was to speak. She had to come back and tell me you and you, (meaning me and a couple other people) you guys are going in too.

Why did she do that? Because one of her superiors for whatever reason told her to go back in and select Vikki from VMH magazine and a couple of others to go into the space where President Obama, John Kerry, Valerie Jarrett, Mark Zuckerberg and others were speaking, and tell these people they've been selected. As I was grabbing my valuables – my cameras, my purse, my wallet – to go into this room she said, "you can't take that in there." And I was like, "I can't leave it out here," and she says, "well I'm not going to watch it."

Anyway I simply looked for a place at one of the tables where I could hide my equipment, asked another woman to keep her eyes on it if she was there. For for the most part, the people who were in the media area of that room, those folks were not there to steal anything. I felt very comfortable after the fact, I said, "you know what, my things will be okay." I said to her and went on where we were to go through security for President Obama's appearance.

What got me was the fact that what she told me to leave behind, were things everyone else had. Of course with secret service, security dogs and all we had to go through the check with our bags but the point is, other people kept their belongings. Which left me even more confused. Although I didn't have my main equipment, I was able to grab one camera, a tripod and my Mac. I'll say this when you believe in what you're doing, even when people are mean to you, doors will still open. In particular when you work for it you know your vision, your vision is clear and you can see - so just go.

There was one other little hiccup or bump. Technology has advanced so much to where people do not need to carry huge heavy cameras or anything like that. The guy behind me at that event was really upset about my smaller digital camera versus the huge heavy camera that he was carrying. This was not because of the weight of his machine but because technology had advanced so much to where the smaller guys were able to get into the room. He made sure I heard and those of us with smaller cameras heard him express his disdain for us with small cameras. But I was elated, nothing deterred me, I was in the room!

Here's the interesting thing, while walking to the security check another camera lady and I were talking and she told me that when it comes to events like this she doesn't buy the huge cameras but she rents them to get the job done for the event. I thought that was like a very good idea.

The gentleman who was escorting us overheard us talking and I think she must have asked me where I work, or something along those lines. She asked me my name, I said I'm Vikki and she introduced herself but the guy who escorted us into the building he turns around and say yeah 'you're Vikki with

VMH magazine of Atlanta'. I was dumbfounded! The guy was from the White House, we were in Palo Alto, California for President Obama's Global Entrepreneurship Summit, and I said "You knew who I am and my magazine!' He pointed that out right there in front of all these people. In a happy way I felt really, really good. I was proud. Even though the other lady tried to make me feel bad and was mean for no reason here was this guy who not only pointed out the work but knew my name and the name of the magazine and was happy to let me know that he knew my work!

Bootstrapping. It works, it's hard but it works none of it is easy but bootstrapping, investing in yourself in other words, works. When you invest in yourself one way or another, others will invest in you even if it's through using your services. Why? Because they believe in what you are capable of doing.

Chasing Followers - Instagram, Facebook, LinkedIn and Business Success

Is it possible to have a lucrative business without thousands of followers on Instagram, Facebook or LinkedIn. Do numbers determine the outcome of attracting consumers to a message?

There is a general thought that one must strive for social media numbers in order to appear as the best or most popular in a field. Numbers are just that – appearances. Granted actors such as Will Smith, performers like Chris Brown and companies like Hilton Hotels stand out from the rest in branding and are likely to have millions of followers, likes and such.

There is an unhealthy notion for small and medium size businesses and emerging talent to chase numbers. If untrained in what matters most, people could very easily be led away from product development with quality to the frustration of thousands of likes and follows.

Is it possible to increase followers and likes while remaining focused on what matters most – authentic messages. Yes, it is possible to do both but companies and talent have to hire a team to increase numbers. But in an effort to balance the frustration of number chasing, *focus on quality* and *creating the best product* versus concern of others 'liking' your work.

It reminds me of a general rule of thumb that I learned as a child – should I be myself or be what others want me to be so they all 'like' me. There is nothing wrong with being liked whether it's on Instagram, Facebook, LinkedIn, GooglePlus however, being yourself is just as valuable. The race for numbers reminds me of that childhood principal.

I must say, it's an interesting fact that before a speaking engagement, a solid contract, or hire that involves publicity the other party wants to know how many followers and likes one has. Yes numbers and popularity generally wins the gig. But there are times when the unpopular and the least likely win the race.

Create Opportunity

Opportunity doesn't always jump in your lap. There are times when we have to create opportunity by working with what we have, reinventing ourselves and finding innovative ways to reach results.

Before getting where I am today, I knocked on doors for work, looking for practically any job that I could get. Looking back, it seems like such a shame to see talent so brusquely spurned.

One day, making my way as though it were my last chance at life, I sat down in front of a computer in the local library. After browsing the internet I found what I was looking for – the employment agency open hours - an employment agency find jobs for people seeking work. Practically sprinting from the computer, I scrambled down the stairs to the main floor. Wearing professional attire and small kitten heels I felt confident that this place would help me find a job.

Tumble, tumble, tumble...'Is this really happening? Am I tumbling down the stairs? I'm confused.' Thump!

The wall at the bottom of the steps brought my body to a halt. I lay there, momentarily stunned, trying to understand what had happened. While going down the stairs my heel caught the carpet, which caused me to go tumble over and over head first down the stairs.

"Ma'am are you ok?" exclaimed someone.

Because of my fall I missed the workforce meeting and I tore a meniscus. Most of the jobs I could have worked required standing or using my legs in some way. Those jobs all went out the window when the swelling and bruising appeared within 24 hours. I could only sit and allow my body to begin repairing the torn meniscus.

With nothing to do but sit and wait for a doctor's appointment, I decided to listen to some tapes a friend had given me to transcribe. I took to the keyboard, listened to the tapes and typed what I heard. Little did I know that this would be a stir for me to get back to my vision of becoming a book publisher.

No work came for me at that time, but instead side doors opened in very peculiar ways. Had I not fallen down those stairs I would likely have delayed the process of putting 'words to paper' – transcribing.

I believe I was not meant to go to the workforce place that day or on any day. Instead, this incident set me on a different path. I was prompted to sit down - due to a knee injury as a result of the fall - and begin the process of book publishing.

Eventually, I discovered the public relations, mainstream media gap, which prompted me to branch off into the field of digital magazine publishing.

My point in sharing this is that sometimes opportunity does not knock on our doors; we have to create it and open doors for ourselves.

You Are Onto Something If Are Selling

My company is privately owned, with no debt, meaning there was no profit sharing or partial ownership of my company owed to investors or venture capitalists. I can brag about that now, but early on I desperately wanted someone with deep pockets to invest in my vision. However, for me, funding never came, so I had to figure out a way to generate the revenue needed to grow my business on my own.

In my opinion monetary investments afford enterprises a faster route to profitability. However, on the other hand, I've seen investors invest in products/companies that went nowhere. So, financial backing is not always what gets a company to the top.

There was a point when I desperately wanted someone to believe in my services and what I sought to do, which was ultimately to bridge the gap between the very famous and the unknown. There are a lot of folks out there seeking an opportunity to share their creativity and ideas. But, the reality is that big business is looking for the 'most popular' because that is what sells. My line of work includes publicity, storytelling and publishing. There is generally not much interest in the nine to five guy working at a railroad company and his idea of news. Rather, people seem to want to know what the rich and famous are doing and thinking. They want red carpet highlights, and the latest on the biggest pop stars. The 4-1-1 on celebrities makes for breaking news and good book reads.

Because 'people want to know,' the news sites and books that provide information about the glitz and glam of celebrities sells the most advertisements and books. Why would a mainstream publisher or other media print, publish or write anything about the guy working at the railroad track? That won't sell books or ads. Strong brands only want 'numbers' about how many people are reading the news at that particular website or magazine, or they want to know how many followers a celebrity has, as that's what sells.

Now, here I am looking at this saying "okay I understand the business side of this," but what about those people with fantastic stories, talent and ideas that are looking to get their product, voice or story out there? What are they supposed to do?

Those are the thoughts and questions that led to my company, a company that's bringing these unknown, ordinary people into the picture by providing a platform for them to have their say.

Immediately I was confronted with this question: How do I grow my company and make people aware that I am here offering a service to them that allows them to fulfill their pressing creative desires?

How am I going to get the word out if no one opens the door so that I can talk about my company? And what about when no one believes in my vision to bridge the gap between the famous and the unknown? I found that the brain is an incredible tool. If you allow it to do its job, amazing solutions to brick walls spring up.

I believed that in order to grow my company I needed funding or an investor, primarily for the purposes of marketing and staffing. My experience has changed my mindset about this belief. I found that the money that you need is out there; you just have to figure out a way to go get it.

I went and got it one client at a time; people that paid my fee for the service(s). This is how I made money. I did not waste money on frivolous things, but instead bought food, clothing, gas, etc. Every penny after that was spent investing in my company. Whether it was equipment, advertising with Google, travel to places beyond my immediate scope to expand my brand or paying for a new hairstyle to make sure I looked decent behind the mic, I put my money where it was needed. This determined approach helped me expand my brand, to grow my company.

My mindset began to change from thinking I needed investors to thinking I could do it myself. I could grow at a steady pace, on solid ground without someone loaning me money or owning a portion of my company. For some having investors means they have support, guidance and connections that will aid in the rapid expansion of their business and a quick route to profitability. This in itself is a wonderful thing; I have no complaint about making money faster, but if you are in the position where no one believes in your product or service, do you just throw it in the trash can?

Here's my take:

If your product or service sells, and each tax season your profit margin increases that means you are on to something. Whether others with 'big pockets' believe it or not, you have to stick with it. Now if it's causing more havoc than it's worth, or not seeing any profit, you may well want to tweak your approach and make some adjustments in order for things to run more smoothly.

I've had to tweak my business on more than one occasion to make it operate better and produce more. However, the one thing I aim to remain focused on is quality over quantity and not letting the numbers overshadow the service. Quality will yield results, if not in one lump sum from an investor, then it will do so one customer at a time.

There are all types of funding sources, like angel investors, venture capital, crowdfunding, business loans etc.

The popular show 'Shark Tank' has been compared to venture capitalism, as each of the shows cast are venture investors. However several of the stars contest they are not venture capitalists but investors.

I've learned firsthand that during scale, I had to keep up with and get in front of my growth or my business will crash and burn. There is no backing off, no sitting in a lounge chair and sipping chai tea and lattes. Nope! Hitting that target market is the goal, but as you near it, you become aware of areas that need more attention, and fast! Coasting goes out the window! Of course, having a strong plan and hiring the right people give you more time for vacationing and actually being able to enjoy your success, but the mind-set of 'backing off' should never be adopted.

Let's slow this down a bit and talk about wealth. Wealth; how is it obtained? Is it for a select group of people or does everyone have access to the finer things in life?

It is my belief that tools are available 'for' everyone, but not 'to' everyone. What I mean by this is that 'tools' such as computers, books, technology, information is out there 'free' to use. Inventions are not invented exclusively for one group of people, but instead for people period. The issue with 'tools' involves affordability, knowing/learning, researching and prioritizing.

I started out as a book publisher, but my work has evolved so that now I teach business savvy people how to capitalize on their natural abilities. People from all walks of life, some of who've raised millions in funding, land on my doorstep. Believe it or not, some of them have skills that can make them even more successful. But mindset gets in the way or they need help with perspective.

You have what it takes to make you

rich – your mind, your talents, beliefs, investing, developing a system and narrowing your target audience/market will get you where you should be.

Calculated steps, removing distractions and thinking ahead instead of just in the moment are also core ingredients to stronger finances. Trending items, such as purses, watches and a nice car are all good, but are they the best investment as you build? Let's say you own and operate a growing e-commerce company selling fashion designed by you, do you:

a. purchase more fabric for a critical upcoming fashion show to display your designs?

b. purchase a new car that you've been eye-balling?

Investing in building your company/wealth would be to purchase more fabric for the upcoming fashion show that aids in branding, visibility and more interest/buyers of your work. The car is great, and you should have it, however, you must remember timing. If you are in the building stage and have not generated enough capital to feel comfortable, it's best not to buy that new car just yet. The time will come for you to live comfortably, if not wealthy.

I am aware that there are people who are born into poverty. However, the list is long of those born into poverty who had the strength of ambition who are now very, very wealthy. These people exemplify the idea, 'tools; available for everyone, whether we make it a goal to find and learn how to use the tools is where the problem lay.'

I used $50 from a friend to start my first company as a fictitious name (least expensive registration), but I dug deep to learn, to find the resources I needed to grow, and refused to spend money on frivolous things such as the latest fashion. More important to me was investing my earnings in equipment/technology that would produce more money. With strategic thinking, developing my skills and testing what works and what doesn't work, I've successfully grown my company. Bootstrapping all the way, I know from first-hand experience that everyone has what it takes to live a financially comfortable life.

Reach Your Full Potential & Worth

It is important that you know your worth. Otherwise, you could end up accepting business deals well below your value, find yourself in unhealthy relationships, develop low self-esteem or never reach your full potential.

As an entrepreneur, I've encountered a number of individuals that did not want to pay the fees associated with my services. Based on my experience and the experience of other skilled entrepreneurs, there are people who try to convince the business owner to lower or alter their rates to meet their budgets. I have two opinions on this:

1. If a business has established itself as providing quality services, meet deadlines, sells a great product, and has ethical characteristics, there is no reason to lower the rates. Clearly, if rates/prices are set by a principled business, the product/services are worth its due. Hence the rates.

2. My second thought is that when a potential customer decides to go an inexpensive route, generally they receive lesser quality in return. The saying, 'you get what you pay for,' has merit.

The above two opinions apply not only in business, but as basic life principles. If that guy or that girl wants you to alter yourself in order to meet their own wants, in my opinion they may not be the best match for you, in particular if they persist. Such scenarios place you in a position of 'settling' and boarders tampering with your worth, your value.

So how do you determine your worth? How do you know if your rates/prices are too high or too low? Below are a few things that *stand in the way* of determining your true worth:

1. *Fear:* For a long time I was afraid no one would want to use my services due to the cost and I would end up with no clients. I had to move past this fear.

2. *Lack of Self-Confidence:* As I continued to develop my skills and produce quality that not only measures up to my competitors, but stands apart, my self-confidence grew.

3. *Peers:* I found that when I surrounded myself with a different group of people,

I saw beyond the limiting, comfortable horizon of the status quo.

4. *Mindset:* As I did research and listened to other successful people in my field, my mind opened up to *how it should be* versus *how it is*.

It takes courage to move beyond the comfort of familiarity into unfamiliar territory where others are getting a whole lot more for doing the same things you're doing. When I attended business conferences and summits in New York City, I was amazed to see the mindset and success of these people. I'm sure they had days when they were down, but overall they had made it way beyond what I considered to be success. That first conference I attended really opened my mind and drove me to improve everything, including my target market.

More important than this is

becoming aware of what I should be receiving versus how things in my life are.

Surrounding yourself with people that are not limited in their thinking, and who refuse to settle for mediocre or the status quo, has an amazing impact on your life, in all of its aspects. There's nothing like interacting with people that live on a higher, more intense level and/or with real strength of principle.

When these things happen, it helps you determine your worth. Additionally, it's difficult to settle for what others want you do. You begin to replace fear with confidence, and refuse to settle for anything less than your real value. How to get what you are really worth:

1. Set your rate/cost and stick with it.
2. Do not allow others to convince you to lower your rates/standards.

3. Surround yourself with people that help you build confidence.

4. Do market research to discover and develop what the true cost is.

5. Determine your target market and promote your product or service to that market.

6. Learn as much as you can.

7. Read books that promote improvement; reflect on and evaluate that material.

Information, understanding and execution are three instrumental components to moving forward. When you have the information to know what you are really worth, you should go for it. It's a sad, and at times painful, thing to understand what you should be receiving, yet not have the courage to claim it. Claiming your 'due/ worth' should not be done aggressively; simply make it clear, *this is who I am* or *this is what my service/product costs*; earn your respect otherwise 'you' lower your self-worth. Gather the information to know your worth, then understand your worth and finally execute your plan to claim your worth! Now you're moving forward!

Without value we cannot find our purpose. A lot of people get cheated in life because they don't know their worth.

Don't Waste Your Time

Don't waste your time doing things or spending time with people that detract from your life. Some people look to take short cuts, and they will pilfer your knowledge, insight and experience to improve their own lives. Don't allow this to happen because you end up drained, depleted and they are off and running on your energy.

If folks are looking for inspiration, let them buy a ticket to an inspirational conference. If people look to you to teach them and not do any work of their own, encourage them to research the topic or go to school to learn more. Don't contribute to their laziness by letting them use you as a short cut.

There's nothing wrong with sharing information, but what do you get in return? Remember, every time you freely share your treasured jewels you are diminishing your value. Your wisdom came at a cost, be shrewd about whom you share it with and don't waste your time.

On more than one occasion folks called my company looking for free book publishing information. One time a lady called me looking for help with book publishing and I gave her my fees for my business consultation. In addition, I gave her my quote for actually publishing a book. She replied, 'I do not have money.' OK, so it's at that point that I knew I was wasting my time. There was no need to continue the conversation. Instead I advised the woman to do some research to help herself.

This is a prime example of wasting my time. Had I given her information for any period of time with no compensation, I would have wasted my time. There is no point in going into a store if you know you don't have any money. Businesses are not in business to give away their services or products, or to take out of their cash register to give to consumers. *Business owners are in business to make money, point blank.*

People who know what they want and are ready to pay for it are the type of folks who do not waste your time. I've learned to pay attention to various aspects of situations in order to determine if they are a waste of time or worth pursuing. You can too!

Believe in yourself.

There are many people who, if you let them, would have you doubt yourself, tamper with your thinking or interfere with your confidence. Don't let them do it. Take your torch from anyone that's holding it and run.

When we take the time to pay attention to our emotions we notice when we're feeling uncomfortable or something has shifted inside of us. Sometimes this awareness serves as a protection from others around us who deplete us by injecting low self-esteem or self-doubt.

For example, you decide you want to write a book, but someone says, 'why would you want to do that, you won't be able to get it published.'

The seeds of self-doubt, once planted, can ultimately tamper with your belief in your ability to write a book. In the end this may not stop you, but it could severely affect your belief in yourself. Your belief system is the motivator for all that you do.

Marketing in the 21st Century

Simply stated, marketing is bringing attention to your brand. In order for people to purchase or use it they have to know the brand exists. I think it's important to understand that marketing does not always mean an elaborate, aggressive campaign running across two continents.

In its mildest form it's using creative content, design or videos distributed on popular platforms or platforms where you believe your audience is. Talk to your audience through your creativity, or even use your voice through video to let people know why they should use your brand.

Don't focus on the competition but convey your passion for your product through 'why' it works, 'how' you know it works and share customer experience(s) to gives proof that it lives up to its promise.

Below I've listed a *few* practical tips and a 'mindset' that will help augment your brand's visibility:

- Believe in what you're doing.
- Focus on people and supplying a quality product or service.
- Do not let money become your sole focus; regularly evaluate your company value system.
- Determine the group of people for whom you created your product/service and concentrate your energy on that specific group, the target market.
- Share quality imagery of your product and things directly related to your product on Instagram, Twitter, Facebook,

Me During Business Conference - I Always Focused on the Doing My Best Job

Actor, Robert De Niro
(NABSHOW NY)

Photo Credit: Vikki Jones

Comedian, Kevin Hart
(At Morehouse College)

Photo Credit: Vikki Jones

Talk Show Host,
Wendy Williams
(NABSHOWNY)

Photo Credit: Vikki Jones

Foursquare Co-Founder, Dennis Crowley (Ascent Conference NY)

Photo Credit: Vikki Jones

Vikki Jones, Founder
VMH Magazine (a print
on demand version of my
publication)

Photo Credit: Garry Jones

My White House Press Pool Pass During GES 2016 Hosted by Former President Barack Obama

Former President
Barack Obama
Speaking
Global
Entrepreneurship
Summit Held in
Silicon Valley

Photo Credit: Vikki Jones

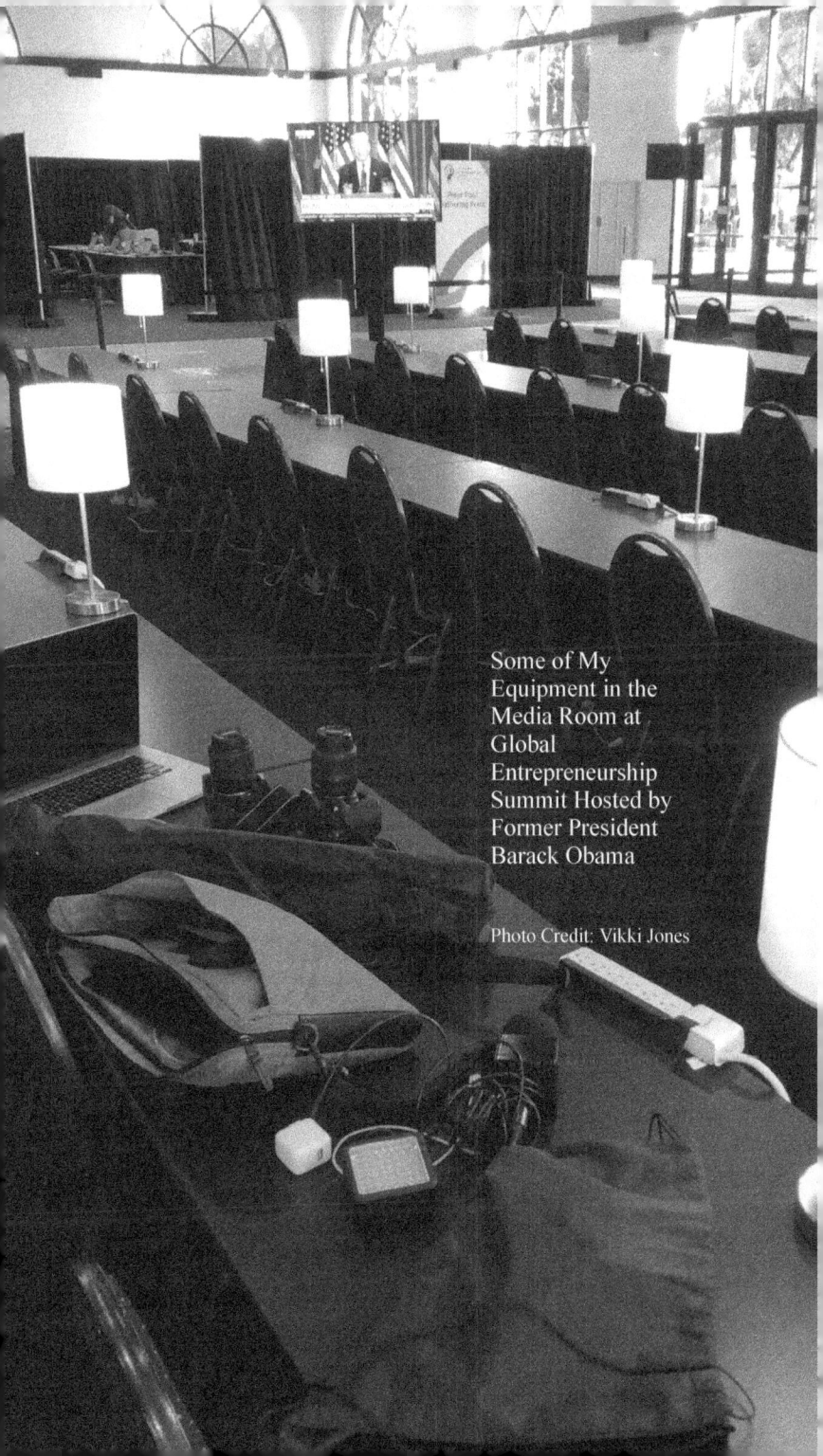

Some of My Equipment in the Media Room at Global Entrepreneurship Summit Hosted by Former President Barack Obama

Photo Credit: Vikki Jones

Inside Where Former
President Obama Spoke

Kenneth Lin, Founder Credit Karma
(Ascent NY)

Photo Credit: Vikki Jones

Mr Kai-Fu Lee, President,
Sinovation Ventures
Artificial Intelligence
Institute
(Economist Events)

Photo Credit: Vikki Jones

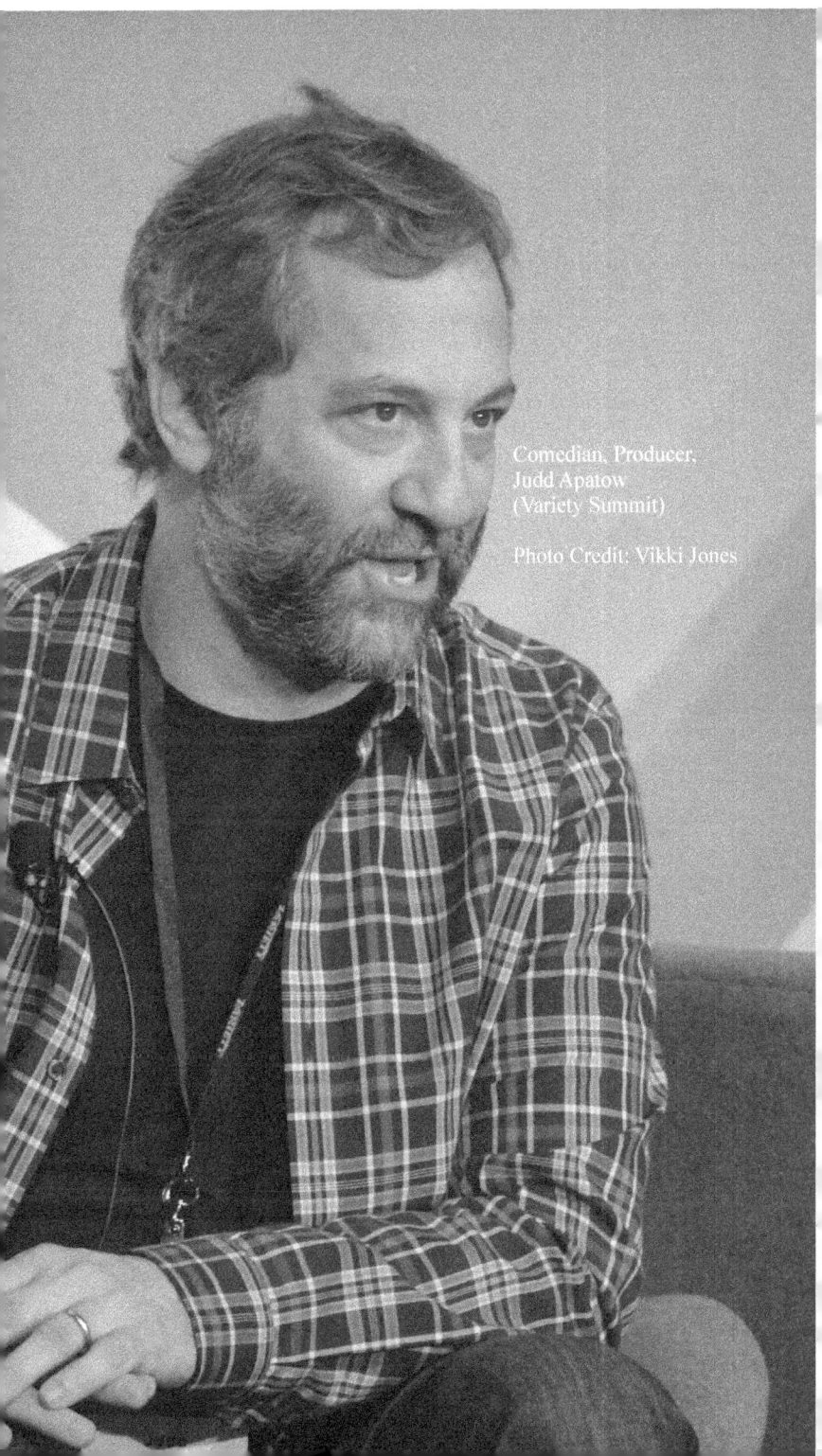

Comedian, Producer,
Judd Apatow
(Variety Summit)

Photo Credit: Vikki Jones

At Global
Tech
Conference

BUILD

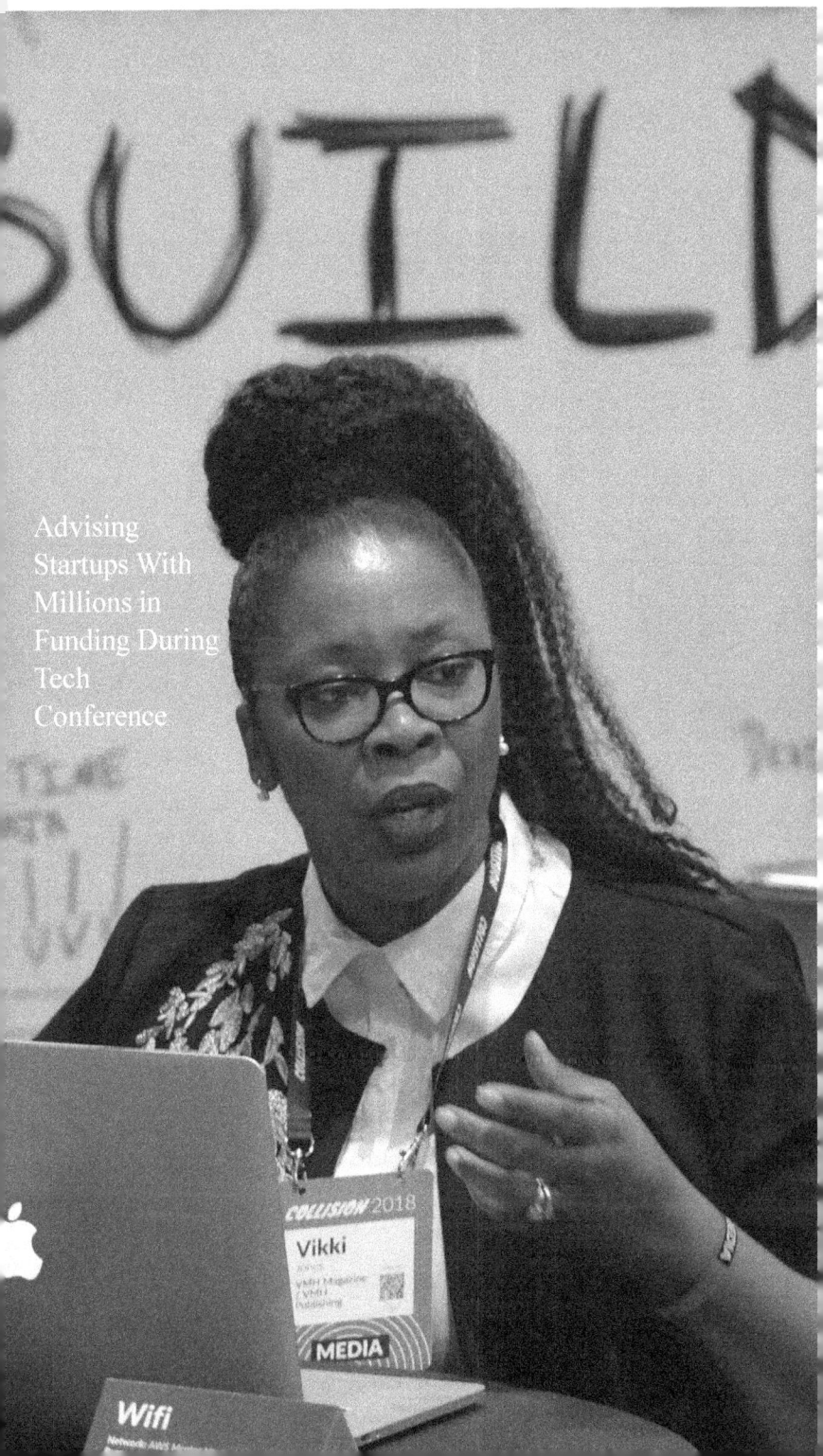

Advising
Startups With
Millions in
Funding During
Tech
Conference

COLLISION 2018

Vikki

VMH Magazine
/ VMH
Publishing

MEDIA

Wifi

Business Hall of Fame
2 Consecutive Years
VMH Publishing, LLC
BOOK PUBLISHER
Best of
2018
Atlanta
Presented By:
Atlanta
Award Program

2016 **GLOBAL
ENTREPRENEURSHIP
SUMMIT**
SILICON VALLEY-USA

MEDIA NOTE: **Global Entrepreneurship Summit Featured Speakers Annou**

For Immediate Release

President Obama will headline the 2016 Global Entrepreneurship Summit (GES) to be host
Palo Alto, California, June 22-24, 2016. More than 1,000 attendees, including entrepreneu
foreign government officials, and business representatives who represent the full measure
from diverse backgrounds across our nation and the world will gather for two plenary sessi
sessions and master classes. The Plenary Session line up includes:

9:00   Thursday, June 23: Opening Plenary

Welcome Remarks

> ·   Richard Stengel, Under Secretary for Public Affairs and Public
> Department of State

> ·   John Kerry, U.S. Secretary of State

Entrepreneurial Inspiration

- ·   Reid Hoffman, Entrepreneur, Executive, and Investor
- ·   Sheila C. Johnson, Founder and CEO, Salamander Hotels and
- ·   Travis Kalanick, CEO, Uber
- ·   Valerie Jarrett, Senior Advisor to President Barack Obama
- ·   Brian Chesky, Founder and CEO, Airbnb

Success Stories from Previous GES: Moderated by Chamath Palihapitiya, Social Capital

- Cheryl Yeoh, former CEO, Malaysian Global Innovation and Cre (MaGIC), Malaysia

- Bedriye Hulya, Founder of b-Fit, Turkey

- Prashant K. (PK) Gulati, The Smart Start Fund, UAE

- Youssef Chaqor, Founder and General Manager of Kilimanjaro E

- Marion Moon, Founder-Director, Wanda Organic Limited, Kenya

9:30   Friday, June 24: Partner Plenary

Partner Plenary

- Welcoming remarks: Penny Pritzker, U.S. Secretary of Commerc

- Cast of HBO's "Silicon Valley"

- Steve Case, Co-Founder of AOL and Chairman of Revolution wi winning entrepreneurs

- Sundar Pichai, CEO of Google

- President of the United States Barack Obama

- Mark Zuckerberg, Founder of Facebook, and three young entrepr

- Maria Contreras-Sweet, Administrator of the Small Business Adr

The Plenary Sessions will be livestreamed at www.ges2016.org.

Actual Email From GES2016 Staff

At this point I knew I'd done well in
growing my company through bootstrapping.

and Google+.

- Create a hashtag for your product/service and hashtags for things directly related to your product/service.

- Advertise online with resources/ platforms that provide content for your target market.

- Create a professional, interactive, 'uncluttered' website for your visitors.

- Create or hire a professional to produce quality videos describing your brand. Once produced, share your video on all social media platforms and embed the video(s) in your website.

- Write a book. Books seems to have become the modern day 'business card'. Notice the amount of books written by very wealthy and powerful business owners. Warren Buffet, Bill Gates, Richard Branson, Howard Schultz, Michael Bloomberg, Mark Cuban and a host of other billionaires. Yes, these people take success to another level, but their books are essentially marketing tools filled with insight and tips.

Okay so we have those, but what about direct human to human interaction, i.e. communication. Word of mouth marketing (#WOMM) is still a very powerful force in the world of business. So, should you place more energy on word-of-mouth marketing or internet marketing?

Word of Mouth Marketing (WOMM) is a solid source of marketing, but if you are solely dependent upon word of mouth, will your business stand out in our technological, internet based world.

For a lot of consumers and businesses, it is difficult to embrace using internet tools like Facebook and other platforms. Nevertheless, it is critical that entrepreneurs remove any fears they might have of the internet, while keeping in mind that due to its credibility word of mouth marketing is still a force to be reckoned with.

Clearly there is power in sharing a one-on-one personal experience, but is the internet the strongest marketing force?

This is an astronomical amount of people using the internet and social media sites. Simply by sheer force of numbers, it is vital for marketers and business owners to implement internet/digital marketing within their marketing plans/budget. There are a host of internet marketing options, so choose those that are best for you, those that will expand your base.

Word-of-mouth occurs everywhere people get together: at the local pub, at home, in the sports club and increasingly online and on social media. - iScoop

Here's my solution, give an excellent customer experience and let others talk about it in person and otherwise (WOMM). Include internet marketing (social media, websites, online advertising, email marketing, etc.) in your marketing strategy.

Care and caution are required when a business grows. Growing too fast or too slow can be detrimental. One may say that there is no such thing as side effects to growing too fast. I argue the point that if a system is not built to handle growth, a team is not in place for scaling at a rapid pace the company could crash and burn causing its demise.

Examples:

- Website crash due to influx of customers
- Product quality is effected

- Inability to provide service/product in a timely manner
- Manufacturer or production issues

If you have created a quality product this will aid organic growth.

On another note, if you cannot afford top-notch services it is best to develop you're own creative skills. Google reasonable rates that match your budget. Either way you will have to pay something as cheap, free of charge thinking is not the answer to business success. Money in your bank account or the lack thereof should not dictate cheap choice or cheap thinking.

Quality should always be at the top of your mind. In order to be the best you have to do the best, which at times means to do the best you can with what you have. I've found that when I do my best, and think my best, the best comes. At times, it has meant redefining best but it still boiled down to quality and successful positive thinking.

Facelifts in Business

Every company or product must have a facelift. For the purpose of this section, I am going to give you my definition of facelift in business.

As you grow, as the world changes, or as your services or product line expands, the look and feel cannot remain the same. One of my many mottos is: "what got you here won't get you there" – this includes the appearance of your product. When Coca Cola and Pepsi Cola started out with their logos, they had the look of 1886. If you take a look at the development of their logos you can clearly see the changes/

improvements of the logos through the years.

Part of the reason this took place is because they had to change their appearance with the time. What worked in the 1800's would not work in the 1900's nor in the 21st century. Like fashion where storefronts have to create new designs, labels and websites in order to maintain success as a company.

Some people resist change, resist new practices and ultimately resist sustainability. Do not resist, take a look around, research big business practices and appearances in your line of business to help you expand your mind. If you're in a position to hire a design agency, advertising agency, etc. by all means do so. It is worth the investment. Innovative thinking gives your company a cutting edge and detours stagnation.

Here is one area that requires a regular checkup and the occasional facelift: websites.

I read a news article about a luxury retailer that opened its doors at the end of the 19th century. It had a landmark flagship fashion on Fifth Avenue. Now all of its stores and its website plan to shut down. It is heartbreaking to see long-standing historical businesses and jobs go out the window. In one of the comments of this article, a woman pointed to the website and its outdated appearance. I took a look at the website's style. In my opinion, compared to current websites, it looked a little dated. This in part may have been intentional. The brand catered to elite shoppers, selling high-end handbags, jewelry and the like.

However, if this was not intentional, the website could have used modernization and an upgrade. I do not press to be an appeal guru, but I do have hands-on experience with the need for upgrades, updating and modernizing the "face" of services and product.

As a publisher, I find that book and/or magazine cover designs give the publication a running start (or not). My creative skills developed as my company grew and I intentionally visited the greatest hub in the United States for book publishing – New York City – I would study their designs and compare them to my book cover designs. The difference was startling enough for me to work on the face of each book through different eyes. The results improved sales and interest for authors and in some cases, I had to revisit books that were already on the market and give the covers a fresh, modernized, more professional look.

Your storefront presence makes a difference and can attract or detract interest. The idea is to place importance on the look and feel of your product on a regular basis, ensuring the best creativity for your time era.

Websites serve as information for products, services and people. With that said, it's important to ensure that clear, accurate, easy-to-read content is available as well as simple functionality for visitors.

The idea is to attract visitors to a website, maintain visitor interest and an additional 'click' that connects you to the customer. In order for this to happen short to-the-point sentences, quality images, and instructional videos aid the process. Use of font styles, bullet points, and knowing your target audience are necessary for website content. Keep it simple when writing for your site, ask yourself: "what should my clients know about my company; and the questions I need to answer for them."

Once this is established simplify the process; make your verbiage comprehensive, without redundancy so your new customer is ready to 'click'.

Publicity & Media Does It Work?

Businesses want people to know their message; therefore, businesses work hard to gain publicity through media.

Although it is ideal to go on a national or prominent local television show and share a message, the reality of advertising is limited by resources. Regular people with small businesses may sometimes appear on mainstream shows, but media companies need to choose material that brings in ratings and viewers.

Why? Media companies are in business to make money as well—media is simply a different type of moneymaker than the product other companies offer. Media companies' products are information, entertainment and—at times—education. People pay attention to information (news), entertainment (movies, games shows, etc.), and education (how-to shows), which means they regularly consume media products. This means that media products gain visibility every time their producers spend advertising dollars.

Media that focuses on people, politics, sports, and subjects that the general public is interested in gain better ratings. While companies and professionals do have other interesting messages to communicate, the key to advertising success is understanding what generates the most publicity in order to implement a successful marketing plan.

In most cases, fame and notoriety is not instant. Some of the companies, celebrities, and products in the spotlight had to work hard to get to that place. They also put a great deal of time into their marketing plans.

For success in marketing products, I suggest continually promoting with the publicity tools you already have. Whether you use social media, digital advertising within your budget range, television advertising, or pitching your story to magazines and newspapers...whatever is at your disposal, use it.

The word will spread, and you will receive amazing opportunities, oftentimes in unexpected ways. Regardless, you need to have a marketing plan for others to follow once your opportunity comes.

Develop Creative Skills

When external funds aren't available or the founder opts to maintain full control of their company idea, absoluteness and business skills are required in order for the business to succeed.

I had to continually develop my skills in marketing and graphics. People are attracted to pretty things be it delicious looking food, appealing luxury fashion, nice looking cars and uncluttered ads. As my company grew and as I continued to study the psychology of sales and marketing I enhanced and simplified the face of my company. On more than one occasion I had to repackage a book/ magazine and give it a new look minus cluttered artwork.Professionalism has always been at the top of my business plan along with quality but quality and appeal is in the eye of the beholder.

My eyesight and views on the definition of quality changed for the better as I traveled to various places to see if what mainstream product/books looked like versus my book cover and product designs. There was a difference.

In bootstrapping you have to narrow down and look like the big guys, delivering big on what you are selling even when you don't have the big staff to get the work done. Strategic thinking, critical thinking, confidence, budgeting, discipline, using earning for company growth versus pleasure spending, sacrifices, strong work ethics, and dedication are all required to successfully grow your company through bootstrapping.

There are no short cuts when bootstrapping. Every decision has to be well calculated and thought out. When opportunities come, determining which is best for the company takes precedence over fatigue and burn out.

I learned a very hard, yet quick lesson during a time when my resilience wore thin. I was exhausted and simply needed direct personal assistance and chose to hire help. The individuals that I hired quickly responded with yes but I soon learned there was an unexpected agenda. I needed to dismiss my fatigue and regain my strength to see the project through on my own without support. This was an important decision because had it gone any other way, years of bootstrapping and building the company could have derailed as I was about to cross over into the company's last phase of growth.

Even tired without the aid of a big team, founders do not have the luxury of completely laying down even when they feel they can't take another step. Removing distractions, tunnel vision, and letting go of weighty situations are all a part of keeping your feet planted and ready to take the next step. So why do people do it if it requires so much? Based on what I have seen their vision is beyond dollars. Instead most of those who start a company, be it through bootstrapping or with investors, believe in something that is greater than themselves that will actually benefit or can be used by a lot of people.

There is a different type of fuel that burns in entrepreneurs. It makes what seems impossible, possible and they don't live/work according to the status quo. They are an exceptional group of people who bring such things as Uber, light bulbs, cars, Apple products and a host of other inventions that better our planet. They know they have an idea that will propel the human race. I am one of those people; I knew beyond a shadow of a doubt that I had to do something about the gap and the cracks between poverty and wealth and literary creative works. That gap needed to be filled.

Technology, Quality & Framework

Using Technology, Business and Publishing - Portions of My Framework:

- Come in and talk - use technology for communication (some people still cannot attach files in emails, or use file sharing platforms). Communication on manuscripts, video chats and website information)

- Although we publish books, we do take a portion of the royalties unless we sell the books directly from press to store. Instead of profit on royalties we focus on marketable, quality, competitive books. This means authors have to set up accounts online, which allows access to royalties, printing and sales. In some cases this encourages learning how to use software in order for the author to 'count their money' from sales.

- Books are product. Most of the authors are informed to treat the sale of their book as any other business operates. Yes, writers write, but they also have to count their money, invoice and receive payments. Again, this requires learning software, technology and at times apps that include payment processing.
- Social media pages for business.

A number of underserved communities from an entrepreneurship, visionary standpoint are passed over by the Shark Tanks. Although this is the case, VMH Publishing ignites the vision of writers and helps adjust thought processes and gives opportunity, which in turns help tap into greater potential, improve poor financial thinking, and replace it with aspiration for a better life out of poverty (i.e., social change). Book by book I literally I have the privilege of seeing hope, joy, accomplishment in the eyes of these writers/storytellers.

Someone is giving the authors opportunity and they are investing in their dream, while at the same time learning new practices through technology and the internet.

In order to reach the finish line the work must have a greater fulfillment – something bigger than you. Generally, this serves to benefit others, promotes change or improvement and brings glory to God's name.

Here are a few things I've found that help me when I feel I can't take another step:

- Go to a quiet place to collect your thoughts, process what's happening and re-center.

- Friends, family and even your spouse won't always see your vision, which at times makes it harder to carry out tasks. When this happens find ways to quietly go in the direction that is healthy for yourself. Later on they will understand why you didn't do this or that at the time they wanted you to do it.

- Exercise as often as possible. Even if you have to take extra walks or visit the gym twice a day. Rest. The mental energy it takes to carry out your vision requires the mind and body to rest.

- Do only what your capable of doing to the best of your ability. Do not overdo it, know when to shut it off for the day to avoid burnout.

- Eat healthy and consume smaller portions of food through the day. It helps fuel the body without feeling sluggish.

- Finally, take a day off and breathe; go to a movie or out to dinner. You'll need the refresher.

Cost-Effective Staffing for Solopreneurs

Let's suppose you are a one woman show, writing, publishing, designing, payment processing, marketing, and handling day to day operations of your small enterprise. You're exhausted, can't think clearly and are trying to operate beyond your capacity.

You know you need someone to help you with the work, but you can't quite hire full or part-time workers to help with the responsibilities. You feel stuck between a rock and a hard place. You feel ready to give up and get a 9-5 and forget entrepreneurship! Help is at your fingertips! Freelancers to the rescue! Your company has access to plenty of 'help' at a rate you can afford. Yes, no matter the type of company you have you can find responsible employees at a rate you can afford without paying the high cost of full-time and part-time workers.

Lets' say you are baker in Omaha with a huge catering job that is not only going to pay a great deal but will also give you company more publicity/branding. The only issue is you don't have enough help to bake the 200 cupcakes, 20 three-tier cakes, and 1,000 cookies.

Breathe, go to Google and research freelance bakers in your area. Also research freelance servers, freelance route drivers (loading delivering the baked goods), etc. Concentrate and narrow your search to your local area or where the event is being held. There is a variety of talent to waiting complete almost any job.

The big bonus is you don't have the major overhead and expenses for those needing more work.

There was a period where it was impossible for me to keep up with the amount of work that came through my company. It was at this time that I hired editors, graphic artists, administrators, writers, and a number of other skills needed to produce a polished professional product. If it were not for these freelancers I would have crashed and burned.

The other thing I noticed is that I was able to feel like a human being as my company spiked upward with new customers. I actually had free time on my hands to live a little, get off work at a decent hour and not remain on the computer all night long. To see my business operate at a higher volume without tiring felt really, really great. Talk about success!

Staffing without debt is not an issue. Jump on your computer and find who you're looking for. Folks are stepping outside of their 9-5 to earn extra income, and some have made freelancing a full-time job. The freedom freelancers enjoy works for them and works for you!

A team must see and support your vision.

Does your team truly support your vision? One of many things I've learned as an entrepreneur is the importance of team selection. As the visionary there are a number of requirements one must keep in mind when selecting a team. The most important part of the team selection process is the patience.

Things like anxiety, feeling overwhelmed and quick, unexpected growth can lead one to rush the selection process. Rushing to fill roles in your company will inevitably lead to disappointments, possible failures and the supervision of self-serving individuals. Those individuals that believed in 'you' and stuck around to put in the work with no pay, are generally a good selection as your business takes off. But, what if your vision/ business is scaling and you never had anyone to believe in you? What then? How do you determine who's best for your company and who's not? One sure sign is if a potential hire comes in talking dollars, more than likely those are the ones who will jump ship if the business suddenly slows or runs into a bump.

Pay attention to your gut feelings. Everyone has the ability to discern clearly, and that gut feeling could very well help with your team selection. Granted, gut feelings and discernment develop over time, but there are times when warning bells go off and we choose to ignore them.

Through experience, trial and error and listening to that gut feeling, I've come very far in determining which people genuinely support my vision and which ones do not. One way or another when it comes to superficial interest or sincere support the truth will come out.

A final point I'd like to make for leaders is knowing when to hire. Hiring too soon ends two ways: letting staff go; or going out of business. Be careful of hiring too soon, it can cause your financial infrastructure to cave in, and can lead to the awful feeling of having to layoff individuals, which doesn't feel good for the employer or the employee. If your vision becomes a successful reality, remember to carefully select your team!

Remember Where You Started for Motivation – My Bleak Beginning

It was early morning., I needed to get up and out of the building before the sun rose and people could see my exit. I caught the city bus out to the mall to discreetly take a bird bath in the sink and freshen up before shoppers arrived.

All set, ready to go; looking like the average business woman, I placed my curling iron back in my bag in the pocket next to my laptop and cell phone.

This routine, with alternating locations for bird baths took place for six months while home for me was a cement floor inside a storage rental - a place I'd originally rented for books and extra items.

Technology, digital platforms and the internet were tools I used to dig myself out of homelessness and into my dream of owning a business.

Business Shift, Mind Shift & Redirect

For many years I worked on a publication that I felt would be an exceptional success. I believed it would aid in the discovery of 'unseen' talent, voices and products. After pulling countless all-nighters, reaching the 'top' and actually growing the magazine, there came a point where everything seemed to slow down.

Pay attention to this stillness; it's talking to you. It is letting you know that it's time to re-examine, to change lanes and go in a different direction.

During this time the 'slow down' meant I needed to rebrand my magazine. I can admit that now, but at the time, I could not. Circumstances were such that I was forced to change the name of my magazine. As you grow, let go. Business shifts start with mind shifts. In order to live your greatest life you have to set your mind free. Free yourself from traditional, status-quo thinking, and envision where you'd like to be, what you'd like to do and the relationships you'd like to have. Contemplate those new relationships and environments; see yourself there and let those thoughts sink down into your heart.

As your thinking develops, your actions will follow. You will no longer accept superficial relationships or unhealthy surroundings, and at some point you will begin to figure out how to reach those new areas. Simply put, actions will follow your newly improved mindset.

I'd reached a point in my life where I wanted to travel more, to have more forward-thinking associations and to put more of 'me' into the people that I cared about. As I reflected on where I was versus where I wanted to be, I began to determine how to satisfy my ambitions. It started with my mindset. We should always make mind adjustments. We should never be complacent or settle. If you're not where you want to be, do something about it.

Complacency can be a dangerous word in business and everyday life. Opening your mind to new practices and ideas is extremely difficult, but I find that doing so is mandatory for truly understanding your true self. Through this business journey, where I have met and listened to many new people, I have discovered so much more about myself. Simply stated, the feeling is incredible. I only wish that more people would step out of their comfort zone and discover the 'new,' 'better,' 'smarter.'

Business Recognition – Branding

Branding is a necessary part of any business. It is directly related to consistency and repetition. Branding differentiates you, your products, and/or services from the next product or service. Branding builds expectations for a company. If people know you are reliable, professional and punctual, generally they come to form an expectation with your brand in mind. fI you build a strong brand then your service/products or even 'you' will be selected over your competitors.

So how does a small business or person build a brand? I am a very, very tiny business owner in the grand scheme of things. However, I take great pride in my work. Below I've compiled a list of things I've done to build my brand.

- *Care:* I care about the well-being of any business owner that reaches out to me. I think genuine care is the catalyst to brand building. Usually people can discern whether you're out for a quick buck or if you're truly working to strengthen and maintain a company or product.

- *Love What You Do:* I love my work! There are times when I'm completely consumed with my work because of the passion, joy, and fulfillment I feel in a finished product. If you love what you do, everything that follows flows. from there. When you love your work, you feel no strain in doing things for others. There've been several times when clients, or even strangers, have clearly seen my love for my work.

- *Professionalism:* I cannot emphasize this enough. I pride myself on professionalism. I always treat customers with dignity and respect. Old fashioned principles help in here. If a customer only has $50 for a $5000 service, do not demoralize them. There is a way to share your price expectation without crushing the self-esteem of the other person. Punctuality, returning phone calls, answering emails and interacting with people all play a role in being professional. When answering the phone or returning calls, incorporate some joy into your voice and really listen to what the other person is saying. I am a talker, so this is a challenge for me, but in order to offer a service, at some point I have to be quiet and listen.

- *Quality:* My skills have developed over the years and continue to develop as I learn more about myself and my natural abilities, but each phase of my growth has come because of quality. I produce quality products for my level and my lane. I don't place Sony, Lionsgate, or Warner Bros. expectations on myself; I work with what I have.

- *Graphics/Logos:* It is important to identify yourself via graphics. One of the things that I have found difficult over the years was getting to a place where one graphic/logo identifies my work. This challenge stemmed from the constant development of my company name. I've gone from one name to the next as I've included more services and encountered a few bumps over naming along the way.

- *Tenacity:* I was once told that I am tenacious. Not exactly sure of the definition, I turned to Webster's dictionary to understand the meaning – if you don't know the meaning of certain words don't be ashamed to look them up. The person that told me this was quite correct; I have never stopped believing in my business. When I started on this road, I continued to plow at it, and even though I was discouraged at times, I never gave up.

- *Research:* The very first thing I've always done for my business is research. Research allows a business owner to develop 'real' expectations, understand cost, determine target markets, and understand the needs for services. Research also allows you to learn from others who've come before you. Research and understanding analytics is vital to the strength of your company.

- *Social Media:* A strong social media presence is also critical to branding. Here are a few relevant facts demonstrating the importance of having a strong social media presence: 1. "There are 2.3 billion active social media users." 2. "The number of social media users has risen by 176 million in the last year." 3. "78% of people who complain to a brand via Twitter expect a response within an hour." – brand watch.com

Amplify Your Brand. On more than one occasion people have submitted photos that negatively impact their brand, preventing customers/consumers from listening to their message, purchasing their product or contributing to fundraisers.

Photos and videos can literally make or break your message. As a book and magazine publisher it is a requirement that all image submissions are high resolution (300 dpi) or greater (unless historical pictures). If images are not submitted with this level of quality, ultimately I can't use the images.

If you want to publish your message with a mainstream publication, it is standard to submit the highest quality images. Whether it's an editorial which requires a photo of yourself or an advertisement which includes images, high resolution with clear, crisp quality is generally a requirement.

When you look at a commercial on television advertising a seafood dinner or the three-course meal that includes ribs, hamburgers, desserts, salads, etc., the food is almost irresistible. Why is this?

After the food preparation and display is complete, the marketing team hires professional videographers and photographers to film and photograph the food, ensuring they end up with high resolution, high definition images, and that the cameras bring out the best of the food through their lenses. This makes the dish mouthwatering. It seems as if you can actually taste it.

It's psychological in some ways; the better it looks, the more you want it. Coupled with a good deal on pricing, you're sold. But understand cameras play a vital role in making the product, or person, irresistible.

Here are few tips for those looking to publish a book, interview with a reputable magazine, television show, look for employment, or sell merchandise.

- Invest in a professional photographer/videographer - don't cheat or be cheap. Research the photographer (check social media pages during research).

- Ask for samples of his/her work before hiring.
- Ask if the photographer specializes in the type of photographs you need.
- If you are unsure of the type of photographer needed, invest in a consultation with a professional photographer to determine your specific needs.
- Ensure the photographer/videographer has professional equipment.

Although smart phones are phenomenal in their abilities, high end photography equipment is made specifically for high end jobs, which are not limited to a head shot for your book or a professional profile.

Even your social media profile deserves a professional look. Not everyone is an entrepreneur but you want to represent yourself well in socializing with others. When you go to church, socialize at an event or attend a dinner function, ordinarily you try to look your best. Well, look your best on social media as well. Fuzzy, blurry photos of yourself can detract from your brand.

Remember whatever you put in, is what you will get out. If you go the cheap route, you will get a cheap result. If you invest wisely and spend a few dollars on yourself, coupled with solid strategy, it will yield results.

Maximize What You Have

My first camera was a Nikon D3200. I used the camera so much it overheated. I couldn't afford the big cameras, but I proudly worked with this camera focusing on quality, while using my natural talent to elevate my brand.

You won't always have the best of everything, but it is wise to work with what you have until you can afford the more expensive items for your company.

In all things remember to focus on being your best and producing quality products and services.

Improvise. There were times that I could not afford the equipment needed for my work. At these times I had to improvise.

I needed a mic flag that actually looked like a mic flag. A mic flag is the little box or circle that is wrapped around microphones when reporters, journalists or media personalities are live, on location, talking about a particular subject or interviewing people. I could not afford the full color printing on the mic flag, so I purchased mailing labels and printed out my VMH logo on the labels, then I used clear tape around the label to give it a smooth appearance. This worked well for my interviews until I could afford the real deal.

Create a Plan. Prepare beforehand with a plan. Draft your plan on your computer or pen and paper. Take time to reflect on whom your products/services are intended for, how you plan to reach them and how you're going to inform them of the benefit of using the products/services.

Whom your products/services are intended for is considered your *target market*. Once this is established it stops you from feeling all over the place, and helps you focus your company on one group of people. Your *target market* is essential to the direction of your business plans.

Learn The Language. My husband once told me to 'learn the language' in response to my concern about the 'terms' big business used at major conferences. That phrase - learn the language - were some of the wisest words I'd heard in my journey to success.

It was mandatory that I learn more, grow and embody myself with people that knew more than I. Of course with any area of growth you encounter new ways of thinking, new techniques and practices and new terminology. In order to truly learn, I had to understand what was really being said as multi-millionaires and billionaires spoke.

Well, I took the time to research the words, analyze them in a way that was comprehensive for me. It worked! I learned the language, and implemented the practice surrounding the 'language' in my business.

Example: I had never heard of a 'venture capitalist', until attending my first business conference. I quickly research the phrase only to learn its an entity or individual providing funds (capital) for your 'venture' (idea, business, etc.). In return they generally get a portion of the return. In my eyes it equated to a loan I'd have to pay back, debt.

My Greatest Tip. Never let desperation take over and drive your decision making. Desperation and pressure are a part of all aspects of business and in so many areas of life, no matter the level of success. Recognize the anxiousness, fear, etc.,s and get it out of there. Trump it with focus, control and opening yourself up to stronger alternatives and solutions. And remember: What is meant for you, will be!

$50 (Fifty Dollars)

Bootstrapping your idea is an immediate way of getting started without the stress of fund seeking. Obtaining funding can be a timely and at time stressful process. However, there is an excitement that comes from investors investing.

In some ways it boosts one's confidence when others believe in your idea and put money behind it. Nothing is more exciting than others believing in the product and believing in you!

Belief is only one part of the equation, profit is the greater thought behind investing. Either the source of capital has to see the profitable vision as a startup or you have to 'show the numbers' (e.g., sales and scalability) before money is put on the table. This makes an idea turn cartwheels with glee but if neither of the above happen you have to dig in and get started. Mindset is the key to any successful venture. If the funding is not coming, switch your mindset and start where you are with what you have.

With technology and digital mediums, you can start a business with less than $200 and in some cases $100. For me it was $50 – just enough to register a fictitious business name and jump on free WiFi along with my donated laptop and month-to-month cell phone. Yes, this is how I began but it's certainly not how it ends.

Use This Space to Jot Down Ideas for Starting
& Scaling Your Business.

Remember To Think Smart, Using Available Tools;
Social Media, Apps, The Internet, Creative Thinking
& Technology Can Very Well Be All That You Need!

_____

_____

_____

_____

_____

_____

_____

_____

_____

_____

_____

_____

_____

_____

_____

Much Success!

www.ingramcontent.com/pod-product-compliance
Lightning Source LLC
Chambersburg PA
CBHW030523210326
41597CB00013B/1005